Julio Hated School

Getting the Most Out of
Your Special Education Services

David Williams and
Julia Alibrando

PublishAmerica
Baltimore

First printing

ISBN: 1-4137-8843-2
PUBLISHED BY PUBLISHAMERICA, LLLP
www.publishamerica.com
Baltimore

Printed in the United States of America

Special thanks to the staff and students of the Pathways Schools for giving us the opportunity to observe and learn.

Scott,

What can I say? This would not have happened if we hadn't partnered up all those years, This book would NOT have happened cause I would have gotten killed!

Thanks.

Julie

We would like to acknowledge the services of Matt Williams, photographer, and Randy Williams, illustrator, for their kind help on this project.

Scott,
Keep our schools safe
and running! You
make a difference for
the better every day!
Good to know you!

David

Foreword to Parents

Over the years we have noticed that parents and kids are missing a tool for understanding and better using the special education system. This process should not be a mystery. Instead it should be a well-known public service available to those who need it. Currently, parents attempting to secure special education services for their child may become defensive and frustrated as they work to gain access into special needs school programming. This defensiveness and frustration may become overwhelming in the face of the extraordinary life challenge parents face each day as they try to assist their child in this process. As a result of this added pressure, precious time is wasted, resulting in much-needed special education services being delayed for the student in need. With this book your knowledge is expanded, and you will be able to find needed programming for your child, free of the defensiveness that gets in the way of making sound educational decisions. This book is a tool for you to use. It's time for your child to begin making academic progress and attaining the emotional growth and wellness he or she deserves.

It is hoped that this book will be a useful tool in helping you prepare to make the most of a special education placement. The information shared in our book will be through the eyes of a student named Julio, who is nearing the end of his school's program and is slated to return to a neighborhood school. Whether you are a parent, student or staff person, you will hopefully benefit from reading this book and hearing what Julio has to tell you about his personal experiences in a special education school.

Most of the public is uneducated, therefore, unaware of the effective special education programming and supports that are available to children with special needs and their families. It is also our hope that by reading and using the information in this book, you will become aware of the programs that exist in your area and how to best use them.

Often children that attend special education schools refer to their bus as the "cheese bus." This term refers to the smaller yellow public school busses that often transport children with special needs to their schools. The term is important because it represents a special education label in kids' terms. Unfortunately, the term "cheese bus" is not an altogether positive term from the viewpoint of many special education students. It's fairly simple to understand this perception as these students explain it. In the student's mind, riding a cheese bus sets you off as abnormal. In this case the smaller, more compact cheese bus leaves many children with special needs feeling exposed, highly visible and embarrassed about their situation. As Julio, the main character in our book, will show you, working through that embarrassment both in getting to and attending school can be very painful. Therefore, getting on and off the cheese bus is a metaphor for Julio's journey through special education settings and services. Our book is divided into three parts: Getting on the Bus, Riding the Bus, and Successfully Getting Off the Bus. Getting on the Bus deals with individuals accepting their disability. Riding the Bus covers students cooperating and participating in their educational and therapeutic programs. Getting Off the Bus explains how a student can make a transition back into a neighborhood school program with the needed supports in place to ensure success.

Getting back to Julio, it isn't that Julio hates learning, but that he hates being labeled. The "special ed" bus is a daily reminder of his inadequacy. It is hoped that this book helps parents and students with special needs better accept and understand the schools and programs they attend each day and, as a result, benefit more from these programs despite the embarrassment they may feel for being singled out for needing special help.

We hope this book will help you to begin identifying your child's disabilities and find the best school program to meet their needs. This book focuses on special education day programs, but much of the information can be applied to other settings such as residential and inclusion programs. It will be important for you to get to know the school climate and not just the condition or age of the school building your child will occupy. If your child is qualified for a separate special education program, the local school system will usually make several school program referrals for you to choose from. Expect to make site visits to several schools before you find a program that is best suited to your child. When you visit different schools you may want to visit with administrators, teachers and therapists in order to get a complete picture of the school climate and an idea of how the program operates. It is also wise to consult other parents who have children with special needs to find out what kind of experiences they have had with the local school system and individual special education programs their children have attended. Don't be hesitant if your child can spend a day or more in the school to experience the schedule and different staff members he/she will be spending time with. You might also want to ask whether your school has enough staff to implement your child's Individual Education Program (IEP). It is very important that you feel empowered to ask important questions about the program in order to help you make a sound decision on placement for your child. These visits are very important in making accurate observations about the emotional landscape of the school. For example, do you find a school where staff is relaxed and happy? Does the staff seem to have a good sense of humor? What are the true emotions on the faces of the students you see in the school? Ask students about how they feel about their school. Do they enjoy the classroom activities? What kinds of experiences do they have during group and individual therapy? Remember, the physical condition of the school is important but not as important as the program and the people who run the program. The appendix also includes a section on parents' most frequently asked questions and definitions of some fundamental special education terms that you may encounter. The appendix is meant to be a parent tool to maximize the use of available services for your child and to help the process run efficiently for the both of you.

We hope you enjoy the presentation and style of this book. It was meant for you to see special education through the eyes of a student who at first struggles with having special education needs but is asked to learn to cooperate with the school. In the process the student is supported in developing new self-control and is able to re-enter a neighborhood school with the knowledge of what works for him, with a special focus on a healthy future.

Table of Contents

Part I: Getting on the Bus

There are some common childhood disorders that can impact a child's educational experience:

Emotional Disturbance

This is both an educational and psychological disorder. An emotional disturbance (ED) is a disorder that prevents you from learning. It is called "emotional disturbance" because one of your natural emotions is driving you. Either you are too angry for the situation at hand or too depressed or too anxious. So anger, depression and anxiety can be real roadblocks to your learning. Feelings are important. If we don't control our feelings they will control us. As a student, if you don't control your feelings they will prevent you from learning and having the kinds of friendships you want. Overdoing emotionally can prevent you from learning and getting along with adults and other kids. Some kids don't show any emotion, and that can be a problem too. If they don't understand their emotions and express them appropriately, they may not be able to succeed in school or any situation in which they have to get along with people. ED can turn into psychological problems. For instance, a person can be overly anxious, which means they are scared of things they don't have to be scared of all the time. Some kids are so afraid of the dark they will not get up to go to the bathroom at night and will end up wetting themselves. Being so afraid of people that you don't play with other kids, talk to them or see them can develop into a fear that limits your life. Also, some kids are afraid of new people and places so that it becomes hard to relax because of the level of fear that they maintain.

Another example of overdoing your emotions is when they cause you to hurt yourself or someone else. Last year my school had to take out the glass in a wall because one of our students got so angry he tried to hurt himself. They had to put Plexiglas in instead. Too much anger may cause you to hurt someone you really care about, like a teacher or family member. This angry behavior is sometimes called "acting out." And maybe the reason you are sent to a special education school is to learn how to deal with your emotions in a safe way.

Likewise, being too sad or depressed can prevent you from learning. You don't feel worthwhile. You get stuck in being sad or down; that's when you need help. Examples of being too sad include wanting to harm yourself, withdrawing from others, not caring about people or things you should care about, including yourself. If you have a "don't care" attitude it may mean you are battling depression. And the reason you have come to a special school is that you need a safe place where you will not hurt yourself and will be motivated to learn again.

Don't forget, the one emotion you don't get in trouble with is happiness. Learning to relax, learning to not take yourself too seriously, learning to laugh with yourself and others are uses of your happiness. Having a sense of humor is healthy, and you won't get in trouble for making people smile. You may have forgotten how to smile. Students and staff need to be able to have a good time at their jobs and if you begin to find your sense of humor you may see the adults finding one too. You have a great smile to let out and make others feel good around you. So don't keep your smile inside! Let it out for the world to see! Joy is like a medicine. Releasing tension with laughter is very good for you. Exercise your sense of humor. It may have gotten weak from all you have been through.

Attention Deficit/Hyperactivity Disorder

The most common disorder for boys is something called ADHD, which stands for attention deficit/hyperactivity disorder. In your classroom there are probably three or more kids who meet the criteria for ADHD. There are several kinds of ADHD. There are the impulsive, easily distracted and hyperactive types. You need to know that the term "disorder" means out of the ordinary. It does not mean disease. So ADHD is a way that a person may be out of the ordinary. He may be more impulsive, easily distracted or hyperactive than the other kids his age. Shaq O'Neal has a disorder. He has a height disorder. He is much bigger than most people his age. But that's just the way he is different from other people and it's not a sickness.

So, remember, if you have ADHD there is nothing wrong with you, but you are different from other kids in some areas and that is OK. Students who have ADHD find it hard to learn without extra help and the word for this help is "accommodations." When your ADHD is severe you may need a plan that guarantees you appropriate accommodations in the classroom like an IEP or 504. Help getting organized, help remembering instructions and help starting and finishing a task are common accommodations for ADHD. The majority of kids find that medicine helps them do a better job as a student; in particular, their focus and being able to finish their work improves. What accommodations does Shaq need to make as he goes through his day? You might want to ask yourself the same question. If you put in "ADHD, famous people" in your Internet search engine, you will get lists of famous people you never thought experienced ADHD. Try it and see the person you find.

Oppositional Defiant Disorder

Did you ever meet a person who always did the opposite thing of what you wanted them to do? There is a name for that kind of behavior. It's called oppositional defiant disorder (ODD). This is not as common as an emotional disturbance or ADHD but can cause you great difficulty in learning from others. If your first impulse is to think and do the opposite of what you are told by teacher and parents you will have a hard time having a successful day. More importantly, people will not enjoy being with you. Could it be that people with ODD think they always have to win or be right? We need to learn that the key to getting along with people is to seek ways to get along with others rather than oppose others. The goal in school is to cooperate, not to compete or win. By cooperating you learn from others, and you change willingly. But if you are competing you are not growing, changing or learning. Oppositional people come across as know-it- alls. And it's not fun to be with a know-it-all. So the main thing for a student with ODD to learn is to trust others with their growth and learning. It must be really painful not to be free to change. You repeat your mistakes day after day. Your special education school is a place for you to have enough chances to get it right. See the movie *Groundhog Day* if you want to see the disorder in action.

Conduct Disordered

A small percentage of students are called Conduct Disordered (CD) because their oppositional ways have become harmful and destructive toward others to the point where they are breaking society's laws. A CD student may steal things from others and not feel that they are doing anything wrong. They are not concerned about other people's feelings. They put themselves above the law and do as they please. They act selfish and lazy because they end up taking from others (the easy way) what took someone hard work to earn. A fancy way to describe this disorder is lack of rule-governed behavior. The school rules and community laws do not apply to the student, or at least they think so.

Some common behaviors that CD students get into in addition to stealing are vandalism, trespassing, arson, robbery, shoplifting, assault and battery, and forgery. Every society needs rules for the good of all, and learning to be helpful and not harmful will help you resolve any problems or concerns you have about your own conduct, especially as you read this. Groups of people need good rules in order to function safely. Imagine crossing a high bridge on your bicycle. And all of a sudden you notice there are no guardrails on the bridge. How would you feel about continuing to cross the bridge? Most of us want to know that the guardrails are in place for us to feel safe to continue our journey. People who don't respect the rules in society are scary. Their life is just like a bridge without a railing. You will notice that your school has lots of rules but the purpose is to help us on our journey and not to limit or punish us. So you see people who ignore the rules make life hard for those trying to do a good job. Remember, if reading about ODD and CD is causing you to have serious questions about yourself, you may want to talk with your teacher or therapist to help sort it all out.

Learning Disabilities

Learning comes easily for most people. Many students have no problem learning to read, write or do math. You may have noticed that there are some students who have difficulty learning. Learning to read is particularly complex for some children and may require individual help and extended practice beyond what you get in a regular classroom. The same is true for writing and math. The official definition of a learning disability (LD) is when a student finds they are two years behind in one of the above subjects. Also, it's important that students and parents understand a LD can happen to any person, whether they are average intelligence or really smart. Some students may find it difficult to learn at the same speed as others. Generally, by third grade, if this learning gap occurs students may be tested and find they qualify for special education services due to a learning disability. When your achievement score indicates that your actual performance is significantly less than your ability level (some people call this your IQ) this may meet the criteria for a specific learning disability. In addition to reading, writing and math disabilities, some individuals also have language and speech problems that slow down their learning. Your academic goals in your IEP will address any learning disability. Having LD also entitles you to classroom accommodations. Have you heard other kids say, "I just can't read," "I am no good at writing," or, "I can't do math"? Those may be expressions of their frustrations that come as a result of their LD. There is hope that everyone will learn to read, to do math and to write. It's a matter of finding the right approach and being generous with yourself as far as how long it will take to figure this out. You will also have to be open to suggestions from your teachers and counselors. Remember, learning is not a race against another student but it is an exercise in your own academic growth. Remember, it's you versus you and there is no doubt who will win. Don't let someone label you as "dumb." Calling yourself dumb is a copout. Talk to yourself with words like, "I have not learned to read yet, but I am getting there."

"I haven't learned my multiplication tables yet, but I am practicing with my flashcards." Just as everybody has strengths, everyone has a little bit of a learning disability in him or her.

Attachment Disorder

People who have a hard time making friends and getting along with adults may suffer from something called attachment disorder. What this means is they have not yet learned good ways to make friends or to trust adults. These students still value things more than they value people. Can you imagine a teenager who loved his tennis shoes but hated his mom. Or a first grader who stole from people's lunch bags and saw nothing wrong with what she or he was doing. These are examples of valuing things more than people. A student with this challenge has not learned the value of a close and trusting relationship with another person. Because people need a close relationship, some kids make up a fantasy person to meet this need. Can you imagine a kid that does not like being hugged or touched? Either you or your friends may have problems with maintaining eye contact, touching or being touched by others or having people look at you. Your school will have you working in groups, cooperative learning and 1:1 relationships. Take advantage of each chance you get to practice your people skills so you can be comfortable around others and help others be comfortable around you. Fantasy friends are OK for play, but they are not reliable in real life.

Developmental Disorders

Sometimes in your classroom you will notice that another student seems really different. They are usually not mean. They may appear to be slower at learning but also slower growing up when compared to you. Just because a person is a certain age does not guarantee that they are mature and grownup on the inside. Your fellow student may be 12 years old on the outside but yet 5 years old in their thinking and feeling. They are behind you and your classmates. In short, their personal development is slower. They have what is called a developmental disorder (DD). As any person grows up, a person goes through different stages in life, and this special student may be one or more stages behind where you are. "Toddler" is a stage in life and "teenager" is a stage in life. The DD student may be a toddler in a teenager's body. These students need love and acceptance and a chance to learn just like you do. As a classmate you can really assist and encourage this type of student. You might think of it as being a big brother or sister to someone who is your same age. Don't be afraid to try to understand and help these fellow students. You may even want to work with your teacher and counselor to understand the specific disability your classmate has. The more you know, the better a mentor and friend you can be to that person.

This is my story:

When I was in my regular education school, I had problems learning and was not getting along with anyone very well. I spent more time in the principal's office than in the classroom. Really, I was angry because I was not being successful in the classroom. At that time I believed that people were making me angry or just did not like me. So I turned off and stopped trying to learn. Before I knew it I was called to a big meeting, and my parents, teacher, principal and many other people were there. You would have thought I had robbed a bank. That was the first of many meetings that eventually ended up in placing me in a school where I could learn. My needs were so severe that I had to attend a completely different school that was designed to help students just like me. This school program was for students who were having problems learning and handling their emotions and behaviors. The whole process of getting into my special school was scary but somehow I knew it was necessary in order for me to find the help I needed. I learned a lot about myself in the process and what I needed to improve.

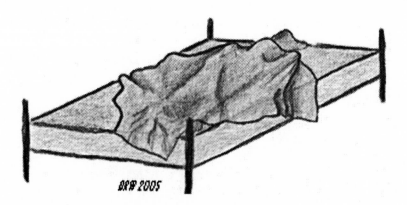

Part II: Riding the Bus

Introduction

To many parents, guardians, advocates and students with special needs it may at times appear that the individual's academic needs are placed second. The emotional disorder (ED) you have been dealing with has caused a roadblock in your learning. You may have experienced a delay in achieving your educational goals. You may have become frustrated at not being able to do the work that is expected of you. Those around you, like your parents, teacher or other family members, may also have become frustrated along with you. Being able to learn is not the problem but finding what works for you in the classroom may be very hard. Your new educational program will not be what you have become used to in your regular school. You will find the lessons and the way they are delivered to be creative and interesting. Your teacher is trying to find out what is working for you. This is called accommodating your academic programming. The sooner you are able to give your teacher honest information about what works for you, the sooner you will discover the appropriate and fun way you learn. Teachers often use classroom tests and assessments to learn about an individual student's academic strengths and weaknesses. You should also be aware that your teacher could modify these tests and assessments to meet your special needs. "Accommodation" means the teacher finds what works for you. "Modifications" are commonly shortened versions of the work that everyone else gets in the classroom. Adjusting the quantity of an assignment does not guarantee that you are getting appropriate instruction. Your teacher will be just as interested in finding out what works for you. A teacher's greatest reward is to see a student who is able to learn advanced concepts. Learning something challenging is what truly keeps a student interested in school. As we said before, if your academic program is taking a backseat this is a problem. When there is joy in learning there is more happiness inside a person because they can see their own personal and intellectual growth. I never thought that I would be telling other kids that school is fun.

During my time in special education I have seen that education is important. If you are not learning something each day you are not enjoying school and it's not working on your behalf. So, do your part and help your teacher know what you need to work on as a team to grow and learn. When education is being done right, both the students and teachers have fun. There is always satisfaction in a job well done! A special education school is like a gourmet restaurant. It has a big enough menu to make all of its customers happy. But customers have to make good choices and tell the waiter what they are looking for. Your teacher is the chef. You are the customer.

You may be wondering what specific instructional accommodations and modifications you will find in your school. Your IEP may require learning help be provided for you. For example, preferred seating, 1:1 instruction, math problems broken down into smaller steps and using calculators for math and keyboards for essays are a few of the examples. In terms of modifying your testing, a teacher may be instructed to help you by reading the test directions to you, and in some cases you may have someone write the answers out for you as you answer. You may also be given additional testing time. These are only a few examples of accommodating and modifying a student's classroom instruction. You can always go to your teacher, principal or IEP to find out if more accommodations and modifications are needed and if the ones you are entitled to are actually being used in your instruction.

In addition, a skilled special educator will tailor lessons to your learning style. Special educators give most instruction verbally. These teachers also know how to provide learning experiences that involve learning by doing, hearing, touching, feeling and moving.

Many classmates in your school may dismiss or ignore homework. This is a mistake because it is an extension of what you are learning in the classroom and it reinforces your learning when you are away from the classroom. Homework also helps your parent support learning by seeing what you are doing in class and being able to help you. Remember, practice makes perfect. Being a student is your job right now, and most adults do some work away from their job, which helps them complete assignments or prepare them for the next day. Do your parents ever bring work home at night? It is like your homework. Doing homework helps you overcome the fear of doing work in class and prepares you for the next school day.

Utilizing Group Therapy

Group therapy is an opportunity to practice your people skills. Let's face it: nobody lives by himself or herself, so we have to learn how to get along with one another at home and school and someday at work. Group is a place to set goals for self-improvement.

Remember how people set goals on New Year's Eve? You will set a goal just like people set New Year's resolutions. But the good thing about group is that other group members hold you accountable to your goals. Your resolutions or goals may be taken directly from the social-emotional goals on your IEP. As you can see, group therapy is more than you may have thought it was.

So group is like a laboratory where you can help others as they help you on the things I mentioned above. A lot of kids, when they start out in a special school, don't want to be in a group and this may be because they don't understand why group is helpful to them. That's where you can come in if you have already been in a group. Sometimes it's easier for a newcomer to sit, listen and observe in the first group session if a new friend eases the way by explaining the "why" of what is happening at group. Just what happens during group sessions?

27

Everybody in your group is there for similar reasons. Some are there because they are working on speaking up. In class, when they are at home, or playing with their friends they don't talk! Others are trying to improve their self-control. Maybe they speak too much. They may also try to take control of the classroom or their friendships.

Another reason people come to group is to learn to remain focused on a task. Having others there helps them focus and accomplish the task with less frustration. Then there is the person who overreacts to everything, usually with anger. This person needs to get a grip on the situation because that is probably the reason they are having trouble keeping their friends and why they always seem to come in to school in the morning having had a fight at home to start off the day.

So, as you can see, there are lots of good reasons for a kid to be in group therapy. As you think about this you may even think of more reasons or situations in which group can actually help somebody.

There is a big word we always hear from the therapists at the beginning of the school year. Any guesses? It's "confidentiality." In a group, confidentiality means that what is said among members stays in the group. Respect each other and show this respect by not talking about what other people say during group.

You may be asked to leave group if you can't keep the secrets of other group members. But it gets more complicated. Mutual respect of other group members does not mean you cannot talk about what happened to you in group or how you felt about it to appropriate outsiders like your parents, guardian, teacher or best friend. This is where the word "judgment" comes in.

If you are not sure if you should share something, ask your group leader first. You will find that after asking for your group leader's advice a couple of times, you will gain more confidence to make good decisions on what to say and to whom. This is called using your head, good judgment.

Tight confidentiality leads to more group sharing and group participation by all members. Trust and respect generally grow in this safe environment. Do your part to keep group stuff confidential.

In case you want to see some topics that my group has covered, I am sharing ten group sessions. Your therapist or counselor may wish to use these at your school. These were my favorite sessions, because the topics were important to every group member. These activities were fun and at times very serious.

What I mean by "serious" is that during group, people begin to discuss themselves and what they need to work on in their lives. After trying to do this yourself, you may then agree that this is one of the hardest things a person can try to do. Enjoy these sessions but don't forget to participate and grow.

My Ten Favorite Group Sessions

Group Session 1: "Slow Motion Charades"

Purpose: To help group members relax around each other in a fun game. The game is slow motion to help students both learn self-control and focus on the group activity.

Goal: Each member will act out a familiar activity in slow motion and group members will guess what the activity is. If you like charades, think of this as slow motion charades.

Activity: The group leader will demonstrate a slow motion charade. The charade needs to be a common activity. The ones that I remember were making a pizza, shaving, driving a school bus, teaching a class and getting dressed in the morning.

Any member of the group can call out what the leader is acting out. The leader must perform the activity as slowly as possible, taking up to three minutes or until someone guesses the charade correctly. The person who guesses correctly should take the next turn performing a slow motion charade. It is important that everyone who wishes gets the opportunity to perform a slow motion charade.

What I learned: I liked the idea that I could take a risk in front of my classmates as part of a game where I didn't know how it would end. Now that I think it over, this is what my group leader and teachers must mean when they talk about "building trust" in the school program. We all laughed during this activity, but we were laughing *with* each other and not at each other. That makes a big difference, because people don't get mad at each other when we do it this way. And guess what? Most people like acting in front of others and group is a safe place to practice your skills. Relax and have fun with this activity!

Group Session 2: "Discussion Starters"

Purpose: We call this one "discussion starters." We will learn to share our ideas and get feedback from other group members. Since talking in public is really difficult, this will help by giving you a safe, familiar place to share your ideas.

Goal: Each member will individually have the opportunity to finish a statement that the group leader starts. In order to practice your listening skills, you will have to summarize what the person before you said and then give your ideas on the topic. It is very important that you stick to the topic so the group does not get off track.

Activity: The leader begins the session by asking student members to listen to the "discussion starter." Sitting in a circle, students are asked to summarize what the person who went before them said on the topic and then share their own ideas on the subject. Group members raise their hands to go next after the speaker. Everyone needs to listen to every speaker, because you want to remember what they said before you speak. The group leader can call on people who are quiet but members can "pass" on a particular topic. Some discussion starter topics include: my idea of a perfect Saturday, the scariest moment of my life, the hardest thing I ever had to do, my happiest day ever, when I get really angry, my best teacher ever, things my best friend and I do together, the latest I ever stayed up and why, the longest trip I ever took, my favorite place to eat, when I get to be a parent, and what I do best in school. Be creative and make up as many as you can think of. Last year I made up three that my group leader used the next week.

What I learned: I found it easy to talk about important things with other people in the group. I found it hard to listen before I spoke and had to ask the speaker what they said on the topic before I spoke. Once I was really listening, I found out that my fellow group members have had a lot of similar experiences that I have had in my life. People are people. Everybody needs to be respected for his or her ideas and for who they are. Those are the biggest lessons I learned from this activity!

Group Session 3: "Bring a Board Game to School"

Purpose: This activity is designed to help students practice taking turns and using encouraging language in a group. We all know how to be selfish and how to put others down. Those things we don't need to practice. What we need to practice is beginning to learn how to talk with people positively, even when we might be losing a game or waiting for our turn.

Goal: By playing a board game of the group's choice, members will learn playing by the rules, taking turns and being encouraging to others.

Activity: The group decides on which board game to play. The game should be played by individuals or in teams, depending on the game. Everyone will want to play. Any popular board game will do. For example, games like bingo, Monopoly, Blurt or card games are good to use. Students may bring board games from home and introduce them to their fellow students. Be sure to follow the game's published rules and make "house" rules before play begins. Remember to be fair, share with others and compliment others often on their play during the game.

31

What I learned: In the past, playing games with other kids was hard for me. I was sure they were cheating, and I never seemed to win. I almost always lost my temper and my friends. Group is a safe place to play games and it gives me an opportunity to talk about the strong feelings that happen during competition. Cooperation beats competition. I learned that rules are necessary to keep people on track and this avoids fights during the game. That's what they call sportsmanship!

Group Session 4: "The Wall of Character"

Purpose: This activity is called the wall of character because it helps you to think of ways to improve yourself one brick at a time. At school your personal goals state the positive ways that you will grow. These are the personal qualities that people see from the outside. These qualities are the ones that make you feel good on the inside too. This activity helps students practice setting personal goals.

Goal: To think of at least three ways to improve yourself as a person during the school year. For example, one kid in my group last year wanted to stop lying and stealing things from people. The wall helped her talk about these needed improvements.

Activity: Each student is given a stack of 3x5 index cards and a marker. Each student writes one positive personal quality per card. Students do not need to put their names on the cards. The cards are then taped to the building blocks (our school uses big foam bricks). Each student places their block in the wall of character and explains why this character trait is important to them. Students should talk about one trait at a time and in turn. The traits become building blocks for the wall of character. You may want to take a picture of the finished product.

What I learned: I sure have a lot to work on and so do the others in my group. But we all found out we have some good things in us too. Wanting to change is really important. You are more likely to be successful at your own goals than at someone else's. This really surprised me, because I didn't realize the difference between my goals and their goals before this activity.

Group Session 5: "Team Building Contest"
Purpose: To experience teamwork toward a goal. Students plan a building design and execute it silently. Students sketch their plans on paper. They accomplish this by using hand signals and gestures to communicate silently.

Goal: To build an original building from building blocks. The building should be attractive, strong and as tall as possible. Students should learn how to accept the ruling of a judge in the team-building contest.

Activity: When we did this before, the group leader gave us an equal number of blocks, paper and pencils, and we were divided into three small groups of equal number. The rules were to build a building that was attractive, strong and high. There was also a time limit of 10 minutes to construct one building. Also, we could not talk during the process. We had enough time to build and judge two buildings. Another staff member in our school served as the building inspector judge.

What I learned: It is difficult to communicate without talking but not impossible. You can learn a lot by watching others, pointing and sketching your ideas. We all seemed to win just by finishing the building. Everyone was happy with what they built, and it was OK that another team won first prize that day. I also learned that just as every building is different, every person has things that make him or her attractive, strong, and unique!

Group Session 6: "Nature's Bingo"
Purpose: We sometimes need to take notice of what is taking place around us. This activity will help you be more observant. It will also help you slow down enough to see, hear and enjoy your world. Cooperatively complete this activity. In this activity helping other group members is considered a plus.

Goal: On a nature walk, observe as many new and familiar things as you can to improve awareness of your surroundings individually and as a group.

Activity: The group leader will prepare a bingo board where the spaces are filled with objects, places, observable creatures and anything else in the neighborhood. For example: squirrels, birdbaths, red cars, white dogs, crows, worms, butterflies, bees, bugs, acorns, airplanes, trash trucks, helicopters and a guy with a crewcut or shaved head, etc. Make the corresponding cards for the group members. The group walks through the neighborhood and the members mark their bingo cards as they see the items. The group leader marks the master board as the walk proceeds. Group members call out "bingo" when they have 5 in a row, counting the free space. A small bingo prize is awarded to all participants. Jolly Ranchers are my favorite!

What I learned: What I think this activity taught me was that there is a world outside of myself. At times I am too self-centered and, really, "it is not all about me." It's amazing what you can see when you take the time to really look around you and study the neighborhood.

Group Session 7: "Memories"

Purpose: To understand difficult and happy events that we have experienced and what we have learned from them.

Goal: Each member will complete a worksheet that asks him or her to remember things from different time periods in their life. Students will share what they were are able to remember and the feelings attached to those memories.

Activity: Group leaders should prepare a list of sentence fragments that prompt the student to complete the sentence on paper. After about 10 minutes of working time, each student is asked to share what he or she wrote for memory number 1 and how he or she felt about it before and after the memory they have remembered.

A few sample fragments include:

Before I was five I remember being happy when…

The earliest event that scared me was…

What I remember about first grade and how I felt

The first group activity I joined outside school and what it was like (e.g. Boy and Girl Scouts, a church group, a sports club, etc.)

The thing I remember most about elementary school that was frustrating was…

The last time I got angry at home was…

The smartest I ever felt was…

A time I felt left out was…

What I learned: Everybody has memories. It is important to learn from our failures and our successes. I seem to remember my mistakes more than the good things I did. But so did everybody else in the group. Maybe I have been focusing on the negative stuff too much. I will begin to turn my negative memories into positive lessons. That way my mistakes will mean something.

Group Session 8: "Value Meal Lunch Boxes"

Purpose: To sort out the important values and people in our lives. We all have an individual value system and examining our priorities help us to have good days and feel better about ourselves.

Goal: Each student identifies and arranges their personal values according to importance. Students will be able to share what their most important values are.

Activity: To prepare for this session the group leader can draw three lunch boxes on a piece of paper or ask the group members to draw their own lunch boxes. The boxes should be big enough to list about 10 items inside them. Label the lunch boxes "super important," "important" and "unimportant." The group leader develops a list of personal values and provides a printed copy to the group members. Scissors and tape or glue will be needed. Students should cut the individual values from the list, decide which lunch box they fit in and paste them there. Everyone's choices will be different. Don't be surprised. They do not have to use all the values listed. It is suggested they paste about 10 per box. These papers can be a source of a group discussion, taken home to share with parents and guardians, or for keeping as a personal reminder of their values.

Examples of popular values are:

honesty	being beautiful
love	athletic
happiness	sportsmanship
maturity	teamwork
fun	health
excitement	fairness
trust	caring
manners	consideration
money	respect
intelligence	responsibility
peace	citizenship
your God	humor
your faith	a toy
obedience	video game
control	cloth
hard work	shoes
friends	brothers
family	sisters
being helpful	cars
eating well	a job
nonviolence	

What I learned: Everybody has a value system. Everybody thinks that somebody or something is important to him or her. That's what motivates us. That's what gets us up in the morning, because something is important to us. I am ashamed to say that sometimes I put "things" and having "fun" above people and other really important values. This activity helped me place my values in better order according to what I really believe.

Group Session 9: "Fortune Telling with the Magic Pen"
Purpose: To anticipate future changes and be accepting of necessary transitions in a person's life. Nobody really knows what is going to

happen tomorrow. All we can be sure of is that things will change. It is up to us to make those changes as smoothly as possible.

Goal: To prepare students to deal successfully with change in their lives and at school. To learn how to make change less stressful and more like a welcomed friend rather than a hated enemy.

Activity: This is a simple activity that only requires a really nice pen with gold or silver-looking trim in a neat color. The group sits in a circle and the leader starts off by going first, so the students can see how to forecast the future. Have the person who is talking hold the pen up in front of their face and talk to it. The group leader will provide discussion starters for each complete round of fortune telling. Some discussion starters include:

With this magic pen, I see myself entering high school…
With this magic pen, I see myself getting a part time job…
With this magic pen, I see myself moving to a new neighborhood…
With this magic pen, I see myself living with a different family someday…
With this magic pen, I see myself as a parent…
With this magic pen, I see myself as an employee of…
With this magic pen, I see myself in an apartment…
With this magic pen, I see myself on vacation…
With this magic pen, I see myself getting a college degree…
With this magic pen, I see myself getting married…
With this magic pen, I see myself adopting a child…
With this magic pen, I see myself choosing to be single.

Group leader should ask members to tell how they will accomplish their future goal before passing the magic pen to the next person.

What I learned: Thinking about the future before it happens makes it less scary. When you look ahead it helps you plan. Having a plan for change is important. I also learned that things change, so we have to learn to adapt. Businessmen and women often say, "People don't plan to fail, they fail to plan." I want to be ready for the things that are going to happen in my life. I want to ride the tiger, not hang on to its tail while it's running around.

Group Session 10: "Spinning a Yarn"

Purpose: To review the group's experience over the past nine sessions and help group members process and talk about their individual growth. Give group members and the leader a chance to comment on the growth they have seen in others.

Goal: To conduct a discussion in a respectful and orderly manner. To help students relate what the group experience has meant to them. To encourage group members to provide the group leader feedback with how to improve the group experience the next time group is offered.

Activity: You will need a ball of yarn. The leader may start the discussion by asking group members to tell how what they have learned in group will help them improve in school or at home. The speaker should hold the ball of yarn and pass it to the next group member who wants to speak. It helps to sit in a circle for this activity. The speaker holds on to the unwound yarn and passes the ball of wound yarn to the next speaker. Nobody speaks unless they are holding the ball of yarn. The yarn goes back and forth as the discussion continues. You can end up with a spider web that is very cool. Eat your heart out "Spidey"! Examples of more group leader discussion topics include:

Which group activity did you like most and why?

Which group activity should never be repeated?

Give an example of a way your thinking has changed since you began the group.

Have you improved in handling strong emotions, such as anger? Tell how you have done this.

Is there something encouraging to another group member you wished to say about their growth during group?

How did the group leader do?

Any comments on the group leader's personal growth over time?

What I learned: Groups can be the place to grow, but you have to do your part and you have to encourage your fellow group members to stay on track and do their part. I respect people more after having worked with them during group. That goes for staff and students. When I started group I didn't want to say anything. I felt that my thoughts and feelings were too personal. I certainly didn't want to talk about my family. But there is this thing called confidentiality that helps you learn to trust others. What I mean is they are not supposed to talk outside of group about what happens in the group. That helped me relax and begin to share about my family and me. I found that I am really important and so is my family. I also learned that groups were more fun when we were doing fun activities, but I also learned to like the talking part too.

Utilizing Individual Therapy

When it comes to improving myself, I have to think about improving my whole self. This work is not easy. Why? People are complex. We are mind, body and spirit, just like a three-legged stool that can't stand up if a leg is missing or one of the legs is too short or too long. A person's health comes from balance in their life. All parts of the person need attention.

My book is about academic and emotional growth. However, it's up to my parents or guardians to care for my physical and spiritual needs too. Good nutrition, regular exercise and plenty of rest make me strong physically. Maintaining a growing love relationship with my God, others and myself are ways I stay healthy spiritually.

To keep in balance, I make sure I do something for my body, mind and spirit every day. For my body I might eat a good breakfast, not just a Pop-Tart on the way out to the bus. For my mind I go to school and do the job of a student. This has been a big leap for me, because I didn't used to go to school enough. In the past I won the imperfect attendance certificate!

School is also where I work on my relationship with the people around me. Spiritually I make a point of doing or saying something that is uplifting to people around me each day. This can be as simple as smiling and speaking to people first. Speaking to my God, to family and others in my life, and loving myself strengthens me. I want to help and not hurt others. I don't want to be just a good student; I want to be a good person too. I have learned that it's hard for many of my fellow students to understand that love has a lot of different meanings, and I have found one that works in school. For me, love is not a feeling as much as a decision to give and serve other people in my life. My therapist told me an easy way to remember this is to think of love as an "action" word as opposed to a "feeling" word. So working on you includes being good to yourself physically and spiritually. One way to look for growth in these areas is to ask yourself monthly, "Am I healthier in my body and more loving as a person than I was last month?" That's where individual therapy comes in to play. As you start working with your therapist, you will be asked what you want to improve about yourself. There are already printed social-emotional goals and academic goals that are part of your IEP plan. You may want to add other goals to them as you work with your therapist. Is your therapist ready for the shock of their life when you ask to work on your IEP goals and objectives?

Now let's look at what you can do in your school to take advantage of the individual therapy that is offered. It is very important that you understand what the different words therapists use every day mean. I know kids that went through the whole school year and did not have an idea about what many words meant. They just agreed so they would not look "stupid." Two of the biggest words are "therapy" and "goals." What I have decided is that therapy is healing the hurts in your life. These hurts are not ones you can see; they are mental and emotional. There are also people like the boy in our class last year that was slower finishing his schoolwork and couldn't learn the same things we could. Therapy helped him accept learning at his own rate and got the other kids in the school on his side to help him when he needed extra support. One girl was hearing-impaired, but she was so upset about using the hearing aid that she would not wear it. Her therapist spent a lot of time trying to convince her to use her hearing aid in class. Students in the class were asked to help her by sitting next to her during class lectures and helping her take more accurate notes.

The other word I mentioned was "goal." A goal is like a target that you shoot at. It is also something you work toward. For example, a personal goal may be to make friends or to improve in math. Over time your therapist may ask you to report on what progress you are making toward your goal. Your therapist will tell you they are measuring progress toward your goal by seeing if you are reaching small objectives along the way. An objective is one of the streets you cross on your way to school. Your goal is to get to school, but you get there by crossing one intersection at a time, using the streets along the way.

Social-emotional goals are a group of goals that are listed for you in your IEP program. Your therapist can show you your goals and you can discuss which ones to work on first. Remember, you can add your own goals. Individual therapy is your time with a caring adult, and you have a right to privacy with this person. Your sessions will be held in a private place. Your therapist will respect your confidence. Remember confidentiality from your group work? What you say stays with your therapist. There are some necessary exceptions to this rule that limit this confidence. One is if you tell your therapist that you will hurt yourself or others. Another exception is when someone is hurting or neglecting you. These are times the therapist will have to report it to your parent, guardian or to Social Services. Another exception concerns your therapist sharing your progress or well being with the school's professional team. This team needs complete and accurate information about you to make good decisions that affect you. Your therapist can tell you as you discuss private issues whether or not they will have to share the information with the entire school team. Asking your therapist in session about what they will be sharing or not is always a good idea. Your goals have to do with achieving positive behaviors, given your diagnosis.

Diagnosis	Positive Behavior
Conduct/Oppositional-Defiant Disorder	Cooperation with a good attitude. Letting teachers teach and parents parent.
Attention Deficit Hyperactivity Disorder	On-task behavior. Self-control. Not overdoing emotionally or physically like being too silly, too loud or too active while on task. Accepting medication as needed help when it makes sense.
Emotional Disorder	Control emotions in order to maximize learning in school.
Learning Disability	Find the learning style(s) that work. Ask for academic accommodations as needed.
Post-Traumatic Stress Disorder	Managing fear and building safe, trusting relationships.
Depression/Anxiety Disorder	Generating more personal happiness in my day. Being positive about myself and trusting of others. Accepting medication as needed help when it makes sense.
Developmental Disorder	Learning at my own pace. Observing personal boundaries of others. Accepting help from others. Accepting medication as needed help when it makes sense.

My therapist and I talked about how to make and keep friends. I had a lot to learn because I had felt like I owned other people. I remember thinking "my family," "my friends," "my stuff" and "my teacher." I really don't own any of those. Nobody is my personal slave, and that was one of the most difficult things I have ever had to learn. The secret to attracting people is to be attractive in what you say and do. For instance, what you say can make a friend or an enemy. It's up to you. A big part of this is learning the difference between negative and positive comments.

I learned to ask myself, "Is what I am going to say to this person going to help or hurt them?" Then I say those things that will help. A helpful person is an attractive person. People will want to be with you if what you say and do makes them feel better. You attract friends like a magnet when you say and do helpful things.

Let's consider the power of the tongue. The tongue is a muscle. Ounce for ounce it is the strongest muscle in the body. It's helpful to use your words wisely. Make sure your brain is in gear before you run your motor mouth. Everybody knows how to put people down. You may call it "joning,"" teasing," "dissing," "disrespectin'," "joking," or whatever. Just remember when you do these things you are on the wrecking crew not the building crew. It's always easier to tear something down than build something up. Your teacher and parents choose their words carefully as they speak to you because they know the power of the tongue. You be careful too!

In therapy I learned how to build others up. Let's call it giving a compliment rather than a putdown. To hurt someone's feelings we tease them about these three areas: appearance, intelligence and abilities. We might say to another kid something like, "You are ugly, stupid and can't do anything right." In this putdown you just destroyed a person when you could have just as easily made them a friend, all by what you said. What can we say to build others up? How to build others up is taught in the "Three Nails of Blessing." The picture shows three big nails. They look dangerous, like weapons! But they were designed to hold things together and not to destroy things. Our tongue is not designed to be a weapon either, but we sometimes use it as one and destroy others.

43

Some examples of what to say:

Appearance:
"I like what you did with your hair today!"
"You really keep your desk looking neat."
"You did a good job matching your clothes today."

Intelligence:
"You had a good answer to the question the teacher asked you in English today."
"I liked the way you handled yourself when those people tried to pick a fight with you."
"I noticed you are able to speak up for yourself when you need help."

Abilities:
"You did a great job on that bulletin board outside the classroom."
"You are a real team player; no wonder everyone wants you on their side."
"You seem to know when to listen and when to speak."

What I've learned over time is that it's not that people *have* these qualities it's more how they *use* them. For example, a person may have naturally good appearance, but it's how they take care of their appearance that makes a difference. It's not that they are smart; it's how they use their smarts. It's not that they are good at stuff, because everybody is good at something; it's how they use their special abilities.

The three big nails remind us to be on the building crew. Remember, nails are meant to hold things together. They can also be misused as weapons. When you want to build someone up, think of one of these nails. For example, with appearance, try to say something positive about the way the person takes care of their hair, their clothes, or the things they are responsible for in school like their desk, locker, clothing, etc. You get the idea? You might say, "You did a good job with your hair today." It's takes a minute to think of a compliment or blessing but it takes a lot longer to take back a harmful word. Some people are so hurt by harmful words that you may not even be able to do a "take back."

Encouraging Others Using the Three Nails of Blessing

Appearance	Intelligence	Abilities/Skills
Tyrell, you take good care of your clothes!	Kavon, you asked a really important question.	John, I am impressed with how promptly you get to work.
Mary, your work looks really clean and neat. I want to put it up on my board!	Byron, I see that you carefully thought about the topic before you started writing.	Julie, you work well with your peers. That's being helpful!
Steven, your binder is well organized. I bet that helps you find things you need.	Christine, you impress me with your math knowledge.	Joseph, your smile is contagious! Thanks for sharing for your positive attitude in this class.
Nicholas, your sweats are always clean and neat. I appreciate that about you.	Jean, you choose powerful adjectives that make what you write about come alive.	Phillip, you are a steady, careful worker. I notice that you take care of the tools really well.
Brenda, the floor around your desk is spotless! Thanks for respecting our classroom.	Rashad, I like the way you work. You are improving each day!	Julio, I want you to know that you have a great speaking voice. You speak clearly with plenty of volume.
Charles, when I ask you to straighten up an area it looks well done. You show a lot of pride in what you do.	Linda, you think things through before you speak. That makes what you say really worthwhile.	Calvin, your sense of humor makes our class fun. Thanks for lightening things up!

    Blessing, complimenting, and encouraging all have the same effect of empowering others to work harder and feel friendly toward you. If you want others to give you their best, take the time to become better at hitting the nail(s) on the head with your comments to and about them. Make comments specific enough that there is no doubt that you care about them personally. Use their name, think of the three nails before you bless.

So I really learned that what you say makes a difference, either for good or bad. You are either helping or hurting by what you say. You are either building or tearing down a relationship. So I choose to bless and encourage people and that provides me with all the friends I need. Our whole nation is really good at saying harmful things and then trying to take it back by saying, "I was just kidding." But remember, sometimes there are no take backs. Isn't it funny the only time it's OK to praise a person publicly is at their funeral. That's called the eulogy. A preacher or family member usually gives the eulogy. I learned from my therapist that the word "eulogy" means to speak sweet words. Why do we wait till someone's dead to bless or praise them? Don't they need it when they are alive a lot more?

Our generation and our parents have become a nation of "putdown artists." You can see this in the family shows on TV. Your parents will remember how Archie Bunker called his son-in-law "Meathead," and Fred Sanford called his son "Dummy," and all America laughed. Today our family shows are full of putdown artists too. Can you think of any examples?

Try watching your favorite sitcom show with this new idea in mind, listening for putdowns. See what you come up with. Wouldn't it be great if we all got to be good at saying just the right thing at the right time and didn't have to rely on putdowns. So get good at hitting the nail on the head and blessing your friends and family. They will feel better and your relationships will get better. Some examples of blessings you can give:

To your parent: "Thanks for doing the job of being my parent."

To your friend: "I don't know what I would do without you as my friend."

To your teacher: "You did a nice job of preparing today's classroom lesson."

Personal Social-Emotional Goals
Owning Behavior, Cooperation and Self-Control

All the adults around you probably constantly tell you about your behavior. I think behavior is your reaction or response to what happens to you. It's the stuff *you* do, *your* actions. Your behavior is your behavior. Try as you might, you can't give it away to someone else. For the longest time I tried to blame someone else for my behavior and as a little kid it made sense. After all, who is going to hold a little baby responsible? But as I grew up, especially when I started school, teachers did not buy my excuses. In therapy I have learned that my behaviors come from my feelings. My feelings come from my thoughts. Sure, some bad stuff has happened to me. What I have learned is that I can choose not to let the bad things take over complete control of my life.

In the past I found it hard to control or understand my behavior because my emotions took over. I was too angry, too scared or too sad. My therapist gave me a system I could use to help develop my self-control. He called it the model for self-control or "ETEA."

He told me self-control is sort of like learning to drive. There are controls that you need to learn how to operate. Every human being has this same wiring system. Learning how to operate it increases the amount of time you are in charge of yourself. The best control is self-control. Let's look at how it's done.

The "E" in the model stands for "events." An event is anything that happens outside of a person's skin. It's all the stuff that happens in your day, like your alarm clock ringing, the weather, people looking at you, traffic, television, strangers, and so on. Events impact us and start us thinking. That's the "T" in the model, "thinking." When an event happens, it starts our brain buzzing with activity. Our brain has three processors that it uses to examine events that happen. There is the conscious mind, the automatic mind and the subconscious mind. The only one we can directly control is the conscious mind. The automatic mind is full of self-talk and habitual thoughts. The subconscious mind is pretty much a mystery. Some refer to the subconscious as long-term memory of past events. But these memories are boxed up tight and we

47

can't get to them. So we improve the most by doing a better job with our conscious or "on purpose" thinking.

The second "E" in the model stands for "emotions." Our thinking generates our emotions. Emotions are our energy for our behavior or our actions and that's the last letter for the model. "A" is for "action." Emotions are like fuel for a car. Just like a driver can go to a service station and have a choice of fuel to put in the car, when stuff happens in our day we have a choice of what fuel or emotion to use for our actions. The four basic emotional fuels are happiness, sadness, anger and anxiety. Emotions are not bad. Just like fuel, they are powerful. You need to learn how to use the right fuel (emotion) for the event that just happened so you will be proud of your actions in response to those events. That's using your self-control.

So it goes like this: Something happens in our day, say a kid bumps you in the crowded hallway. You turn around and hit him. Then you have to pay the consequences for fighting at school. You may defend yourself by blaming the other student, but it was your fist that hit him. He did not have control over what you did. And he has no strings attached to you. You are not his puppet. It may seem like he made you mad but there's a lot more to it.

Think of the model ETEA. What was the event? He bumped me. What thoughts inside of you were triggered by the event? In other words what were you telling yourself right at the moment he was bumping you? Your automatic mind was probably at work saying things like, "He pushed me," "He's mean," "He hates me," "He's trying to hurt me," "I was here first," "He's rude," and "I'll show him." In other words, your brain reacted with a set of thoughts that were habitual. You were not in charge of what you were thinking but it was still your thinking. That kind of thinking generated the anger in your system. With your anger, you hit the kid. It all happened in probably less than a second. Let's see what would happen if you used the ETEA model to change your behavior.

Model for Self-Control

E ⟹ T ⟹ E ⟹ A

V	H	M	C
E	I	O	T
N	N	T	I
T	K	I	O
S	I	O	N
	N	N	S
	G	S	

The event happens. A student bumps you. Instead of reacting with only automatic thinking, you deliberately talk to yourself in your conscious mind. You might say, "He's inconsiderate," "He's in a hurry," "The hallway's crowded," "He's not thinking of others," "I'm glad I don't act that way," "His bumping me was probably an accident," "I'm going to let it go" or, "I don't want to have this hassle today."

You just used your conscious mind to override the automatic stuff you were already telling yourself. The emotion you generate keeps you peaceful, and you are able to say to the rude student, "Go ahead, I'm not in as big of a hurry as you are," and smile. There was no anger, there was no fight and you avoided trouble by using self-control. The point is that when bad stuff happens we have a choice in how we think about it, what we feel and what we do, our actions. So our behavior is really *our* behavior.

This is a story my therapist told me about his family. He was at the doctor's office with his two sons, Randy and Matt. Randy was 10 years old and Matt was 8. The doctor was examining the boys for a sore throat. While they were being seen, the nurse asked their dad if it would be OK to give the boys a "Dum-Dum" sucker when they came out of the doctor's office. Dad said, "Yes, that would be fine." As they came out from the examining room, the nurse offered Randy a sucker from a plastic container full of them. Randy looked at the suckers and asked, "Do you have lime?" Randy took a lime sucker, pulled the cover off of it and popped it in his mouth, smiling and saying, "Thank you," as he did.

Then the nurse took the same container of suckers over to Matt. She asked if Matt would like a sucker. He looked at the suckers and frowned at the nurse and said, "No thank you!" The nurse said, "Well, excuse me," and put the suckers back on her desk. When the dad got his boys to the car, he turned to Matt and asked, "What were you telling yourself when that nurse offered you those suckers?" Matt got that same frown on his face and blurted out, "That woman's a nurse, and she's supposed to help you, not hurt you! I know she knows those suckers are full of sugar, and sugar causes diabetes, and Grandma is blind because she ate too much sugar. And, it spoils your appetite. We haven't had supper yet! She's supposed to help you, not hurt you!"

One year later the dad had his son Matt back at the same doctor's office, but by himself this time. As Matt was seeing the doctor, the nurse, remembering the frown from the year before, asked the dad, "Do I dare offer him a sucker this time?" Dad said, "Sure, let's see what happens." So when Matt came out of the doctor's office, the nurse carefully offered him a "Dum-Dum" sucker. This time Matt said, "Have you got lime?" He took a sucker, put it in his shirt pocket, smiled and told the nurse, "Thank you very much." When the dad got to the car, he asked, "Matt, now what are you telling yourself about those suckers?"

As soon as the dad said the word "suckers," Matt got a smile on his face and said, "Dad, you don't understand. You see. If Randy were someplace and saw something I liked, he would get it for me. That's what brothers are for. And lime is Randy's favorite flavor anything." There is a moral to this story. I hope you were thinking of ETEA as I told the story. The moral is, "It's not the Dum-Dum suckers that life gives you, but what you tell yourself about the suckers that makes all the difference in your behavior.

Model for Cooperation

Do you want to get off the cheese bus? Then you need to learn a skill that you can use with your parents, teachers and future bosses. This skill is the ability to cooperate with whoever is your boss. Learn the art of cooperation.

Everybody has a boss. Even the president of the U.S.A. has people that can tell him what to do. The Congress can stop paying him, and the Supreme Court can lock him up. The voters can impeach him. And his wife can send him to the local 7-Eleven for bread and milk. So get used to the idea of having a boss. It is part of life.

Our first set of bosses is our parents. Later we meet teachers and finally bosses at work. The sooner we learn to cooperate and stop giving our bosses a hard time, we will make progress at our personal goals and get off the cheese bus. In other words, we need to let parents parent, teachers teach and bosses boss.

There are two words that scare kids. They both have four letters and are very familiar to you. The first starts with a "W" and ends with a "K." Can you guess the word? Your parents and teacher are always trying to get you to do this. Did you guess yet? The word is "work." You will need to learn not to fear this word but to expect it.

The second scariest word for kids starts with an "O" and ends with a "Y." How are you doing on guessing this one? It's a word that means we do what we are told by our parents, teachers or bosses. The word is "obey." If you can do the work you are told to do with a good attitude, then you are cooperating. Cooperation is a word that means "work together." In this book we are talking about working with the people who have authority over you.

So let's learn a model for cooperation. This is also something I learned in individual therapy. The purpose of the model is to help us work smoothly in relating to our parents and our teachers. The best part about this model is that it provides a chance to express yourself and be heard by the people in charge around you. The model is simple to learn, but hard to do. This cooperation model consists of the letters COQ. The "C" stands for "command." This is something parents, teachers and bosses are supposed to do. It's means to tell someone what to do. The "O" stands for "obey." To obey means to do what you are told with a good attitude. The "Q" stands for "question." This is an opportunity for you to ask questions of your boss after you have obeyed him or her.

Here's how it works. Your parent gives you a command. For example, "Take out the trash." You first remember COQ. Did I just hear a command? If so my job is to obey it first and question it later if I need to. Now, I stop what I was doing and take out the trash. If for some reason I have a problem with the command to take out the trash, hopefully my parent will be available to talk with me later. However, this may not always be true. Then what do I do? There are a couple of ways I can deal with this. Sometimes I write a note to my parent about how I felt about doing the thing I had to do. Or, maybe I talk with my therapist or another trusted adult about my feelings and ways to work on being heard. This saying may also help: "Kids don't always have to have their way, but they have to have their say." Parents, are you listening too?

But let's just for the moment assume that your parent is open to listening to your concerns. The "Q" part of this model doesn't just stand for questions. It's a time to share your ideas about how to do things better, give suggestions, offer criticism, gripe or just say, "It's not fair." The problem is that in real life we usually put the "Q" in the wrong place in this model. Instead of COQ we do CQO. And questioning before you obey creates a battlefield with your parent, teacher or any other person in charge of you at the moment.

We all want to be the boss. But that is competition, not cooperation. No one can be his or her own mama! You would make Ripley's Believe It or Not if you were. So we have to let parents parent and teachers teach. And it's up to us to get COQ started in the right order. You don't want a battlefield at home or at school. Think about it. What happens on a real battlefield? People get hurt. People on both sides get hurt. And no one has fun. So be the one to cooperate first and smooth out your relationships at home and at school. Work on being a good cooperator. Listen for commands. Obey with a good attitude. Ask your questions or give your suggestions after obeying.

You probably don't realize this now, but this model may be the most important one in this book. Why? Well, adults who are going to make the decisions about whether you get off the cheese bus are likely to look closely at your ability to cooperate. They may not have the time or energy to figure out "how" you are thinking about something, "why" you are doing this or that and so on. What they will look for is, can you do what you are told with a good attitude? If you find yourself following commands successfully, 7 out of 10 times on your self-evaluation sheet, over one school semester, I would bet your chances of getting off the cheese bus would skyrocket. I've only seen four kids since I've been in school get off the cheese bus (and that includes me next year!) and all of us finally learned to do what we were told by adults and cooperated with our school program, parents and guardians. Good luck! You can do it too!

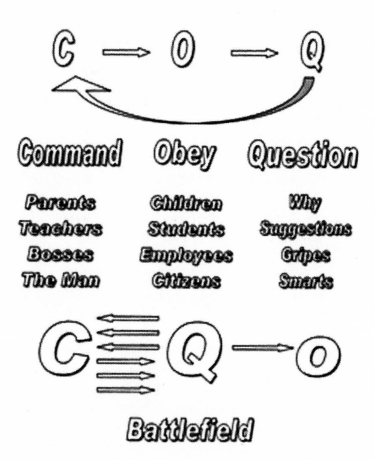

Model for Cooperation

C → O → Q

Command **Obey** **Question**

Command	Obey	Question
Parents	Children	Why
Teachers	Students	Suggestions
Bosses	Employees	Gripes
The Man	Citizens	Smarts

C ⇇ Q → O

Battlefield

The Four-Year-Old Who Would Be King

My therapist told me this true story about a bossy four-year-old boy whom nobody wanted. The grandparents brought the child to see the therapist. They asked the question, "How do you give a kid over to the state?" The grandparents were so tired of battling this child that they were ready to give up. His natural parents had already given guardianship to the grandparents. And now the grandparents wanted to quit on him. The grandparents shared that the child never did anything he was told. He wanted to be the boss of his grandparents. The therapist asked to see the child alone. The child came into the therapist's office, sat in the biggest chair and announced he wasn't going to talk. The therapist began by saying, "I understand you want to be the boss in your family." The kid quickly responded, "Not just my family, but I want to be king." The therapist said, "Oh, you want to be president of our country? We don't have a king." The four-year-old replied, "Not just this country, I want to be king of the whole world!" The therapist replied, "I can see how it would be hard to get you to cooperate if you think you should be king."

It required almost two years of therapy before this child gave up the idea of ruling the world. He eventually understood that he needed to let his parents, grandparents and teachers direct his life. This child had been spending all of his time on the battlefield with his parents and grandparents. He began to do better when he understood that he could benefit from being a cooperator and obeying adults with a good attitude. He got the idea of COQ.

It's OK to Obey

A twenty-year-old man came to see a therapist in his office. We will call the man John. John shared with the therapist that he just got fired from his job. The therapist asked, "People get fired every day. Why did you come to a therapist?" John replied, "This was my seventeenth job in two years. I was fired from them all. I think the problem is me." The therapist asked him to describe his most recent job. John said, "That's easy. It happened today. I started this morning at an auto repair shop here in town. You see, I am a mechanic. Ever since high school I have had mechanic jobs. Today I was fired after four hours on the job. It all began when the boss gave me two cars to work on. He told me to work on the Chevy first, the Ford second. The boss left me. I looked at the Chevy and realized it would take me more time than the Ford. "And besides," I told myself, "I like working on Fords more than Chevys." I backed out the Chevy and began working on the Ford first. You see, I was telling myself that since the Chevy would take more time, and I would have to look up stuff in the manual, I would do the quick job first.

About an hour later the boss came out of the front and asked me why I wasn't working on the Chevy. I started to explain, but he cut me off. He got red in the face, raised his voice and said, "You made me into a liar." He explained that the owner of the Chevy was waiting in his office. The boss said he had told the man that we would work on his car first. And I hadn't even started his car. The boss did not want to hear my excuses about what I was telling myself. I told the boss that he should have told me the man was waiting for the car. The boss quickly told me that he didn't have time to tell his mechanics all the reasons behind the commands he gives them. I remember he said, "I have 10 mechanics. If I had to tell them what to do and why I wanted them to do it in a certain order, then I would spend all my time talking to my mechanics instead of talking to customers about bringing their cars in for repairs." Then the boss fired me and told me to leave at noon. So here I am.

The therapist asked John if there was a pattern in this and other jobs? John said that he always tried to outsmart and out-think his bosses. He never just tried to do what they said. The therapist taught him the COQ model. John realized he had been on the battlefield too many times at work and it cost him his job each time. Instead of trying to compete with his bosses, he learned it was okay to cooperate with them. Feeling encouraged, John made up a rap song as he was leaving the therapist's office that goes like this, "It's okay to obey, it's okay to obey…" This is not the end of John's story. It's just the beginning.

The therapist received a phone call from John four years later. John said, "Remember me?" The therapist said, "John who?" John replied that he was the guy fired from 17 jobs in two years and then he rapped, "It's ok to obey."

"Oh, yeah," the therapist said, "I haven't heard from you in a long time." John said, "I have been working at the same job for four years and something pretty special happened today. I am still a mechanic but the boss wanted to pick a new service manager and guess who he picked?" And the therapist said, "Tell me." John said, "I am the new service manager. I now have 15 mechanics working for me."

The therapist said, "Congratulations. How did you do it?" John said, "COQ! In fact, I made a chart of COQ on my computer at work. I plan to teach it to all my employees. I want them to cooperate, not to compete with me. I learned to let my boss be the boss and today I am the boss as a result."

This story really happened, but it is very unusual for somebody to learn a lesson so quickly. Many kids and even some adults have not learned how to cooperate with their bosses. Just remember what John said, "It's okay to obey! It's okay to obey!"

Discipline in a Special Education School

The disciplinary process is much more involved in a special education program. It's not like a regular education school where you usually go from 0 to 100 miles per hour all at one time. What we mean by this is that in a regular education school you may need to engage in a very serious acting-out incident in class to be sent to the principal's office. It is different in special education settings. In the majority of special education schools there is a step-by-step process to manage a student's behavior. The initial steps are self-imposed such as a personal time out, followed by moderate steps like the teacher directing your behavior by telling you directly what they want you to do. Continued disruption may lead to removal from the classroom for one or more periods. One of the major goals in a special education school should focus on the student learning about his or her own behavior and what it takes to do a better job in the classroom.

Behavior Management Systems
How Students Can Successfully Negotiate Them:

Behavior management systems (BMS) are structured to help staff observe and modify a child's behavior. Think of it as getting on a highway to better classroom behavior. Your school will take time to explain to you the behavior system that is used. However, it may take several weeks for you to learn all of the ins and outs of how the system works. These plans usually break behavior down so you can look at it from one period to the next during your school day. A good behavior management plan will track your behavior throughout the course of the day. The data that is recorded on the plan will be used to tell you how you are doing. Your teacher, therapist, principal and parents can refer to the plan and know right away what's happening in the classroom. A good behavior management plan will show the good things you are accomplishing as well as things you need to improve on even how you are misbehaving.

There are several different approaches that schools may take to developing your behavior management plan. For example, many schools use daily point sheets to track behavior. Other schools may use individual behavioral contracts or checking accounts filled with reward dollars to track your behavior. These documents will state a behavioral goal and how you're doing at achieving it. For instance, my school observes every student for four things: self-control, cooperation, responsibility and participation. Individual contracts may have personal or additional goals. This type of goal might be written down as improving your language by not putting people down. In this example your goal may be stated in the positive by saying you will encourage others. Part of the behavior system is providing students with ideas as to how they can change their own behavior.

You may have also heard of time-outs. Time-outs are also used in a regular classroom. At our school you can take a self time-out or the teacher may direct you to take a time-out. Either way, the time should be used to think about what you have done and help you decide how to regain control by making better choices.

What you probably don't have in your school is a resource room. Some students call the resource room a suspension area or even the jail. When a time-out is not enough, you probably will be sent to a special room or area where school staff will help you first regain control and then talk with you about what happened so you will make better choices in the future. Depending on how serious your behavior was, you may require what's called an intervention or re-entry conference before you rejoin your regular class. Re-entry conferences are types of meetings where you talk with other people at your school that are involved in the incident. Usually both students and staff are involved if they have information about the incident. The purpose of the conference with all the "players" is to support one another in helping you do a better job the next time a similar event happens. Additionally, a good behavior system allows other options to you, such as filling out an appointment slip to see your therapist. Working with staff can help you to find ways of changing the faulty thinking that got you into the hot soup in the first place. Talking to your therapist and sometimes calling your parent or guardian at home or work may also help you out when a crisis is nagging at you.

There is also the idea of following up to see if your behavior has changed or you have learned from what has happened to you. A follow-up meeting with you, your therapist or another staff person should help you see if your behavior has improved. If you learn you have not improved, it is a good time to come up with a different approach or plan. If at first you don't succeed try, try again.

A good behavior management system is going to be effective the more responsibility students take for changing their own behavior. Teachers have already been to school and so have your parents. What we know is that behavior management systems are about you, what you do in school and the choices you make each day. You need to be the expert on how to use the daily point sheet. It's like your parents using their checkbook by knowing how much money is the bank. Your parents know that if there is not money in their checking account, deciding how hard and long they need to work to get the money they need has to be figured out first. Your point sheet is a guide for you. It tells you what your behavior looks like and what you need to change about it. Your success in using your school's behavior management system depends on your efforts.

Most behavior plans have levels like 1,2,3,4. Improving means steps up the ladder until you are at the top. It's pretty simple. A good behavior management plan is as simple as 1,2,3. Either you had a successful day according to your plan, or you didn't. Magical thinking on your part, which tells you that the negative behaviors and choices you are making should get you by, won't work well. Remember, your overall performance is related to how well you understand your school and its procedures, your job in life right now.

DRW 2005

Part III
Successfully Getting
Off the Bus

What is getting off the bus? After successfully riding the bus you are now thinking, "What's next?" You probably thought it was as simple as going to a new, regular education school in your neighborhood. This is partially true but there are some in between steps that you will need to complete in order to get there. One of the most important steps involves your IEP transition plan. A transition plan describes the steps that you will take as you leave a special education program and reenter a community school or graduate from high school and begin living on your own as an adult. This plan is usually finalized at your IEP annual review meeting. Students 14 and older, with an IEP, are required to have this plan.

A transition plan is also aimed at helping you live safely and productively in your community and to use your school experience most effectively. This plan will be practical, leading you to move from school to work to living independently. The adults in your life will sit down with you and look ahead to see what your needs are and how to best meet them. The law requires that your parents work with the school to develop this plan to help you make this move successfully.

In your current placement you have found what works for you to help you make progress as a student. Your transition plan will pass this information on to your next school and future employers. It will also be a way for you to let people around you know what supports you think you need at school and in your community to continue your personal growth. Get ready to trade in the little bus in for the big bus! Oh, by the way, kids who ride the big bus call them "cheese wagons"!

Another important step involves how you are going to get to your new school, who will be there to support you and what your new school schedule and program will look like. The first thing that may happen is that you will be referred to a school by the local education agency during the year-end IEP meeting. One thing you may want to do is visit new schools with your parents and to talk with the students and teachers to find out if the school is a place that will fit your needs.

As we said before, getting off the bus and into your new school is not as simple as walking through the door in September. There is a part of the process that requires you to really sit back and think about not only the progress you have made up to this point but also about what goals you want to set for yourself at your new school. It's a matter of showing the people around you that you are ready to make the leap. For example, you will need to make a personal inventory of your progress and talk this over with your parents and the staff at school. You therapist will be able to help you think through the personal changes you have made and your readiness for transition. They may ask you what goals you achieved in the past and what academic and social-emotional goals you still need to work on. Ask yourself, "Why do I want to be in a regular school?" List some goals that will motivate you in a new school setting. For example, "I want to play sports," " I want to be a member of the school marching band" or "I want a real high school diploma" are a few ideas I have seen other kids use to motivate themselves. In my case, I'm thinking about how I can make new friends at school and in my neighborhood. I also want to remember that school is necessary for what I want to do in the future. I know that whatever I do after high school, my education will be very important. Did you know that high school graduates make three times the income of people who do not get a high school diploma or equivalency? That means that the kid without a diploma may start at a job paying $10,000 and the high school graduate could make as much as $30,000 per year. You do the math.

You need to take the necessary steps to activate your plan. What steps are necessary to get off the bus?

You will find below two checklists of steps to help you make a successful transition to your new school.

Gathering assessments from outside sources:
Site visits to potential school placements
Talk with peers
Talk with parents
Talk with school staff

Self-assessment/setting future goals and measuring current progress:
Using a point sheet survey for a semester to assess your progress
Reviewing your attendance for the school year
Reviewing your grades for the school year
Reviewing your progress on your social-emotional personal and academic goals

There are also some questions you may want to ask yourself in deciding if you are ready to successfully transition into a regular education school:

Have you learned to obey adults by showing a good attitude and successfully completing the "job" of a student during the school year?

Were you able to demonstrate self-control by owning your own feelings and behavior?

Have you made a backup plan that will help you obtain the support you will need when you move to a new school?

Are you willing to move into a new environment that is less structured and where you have to be more independent?

Using What You Have Learned:
Action Steps as You Climb on the Big Bus

Congratulations! You learned some important steps to get off the cheese bus and on to your regular school bus. The three parts of this book have presented what you did to get on the cheese bus, how to make the best of your special education school and how to transition to a regular school. Our intent has been to help you learn, grow and change the way you think and act. School in itself is important but not as much as feeling like you are a worthwhile person. Your time in a therapeutic special education program has focused on academic and behavioral growth. Actually, the kind of person you are on the inside is more important than what you carry around in your head. Believe that you matter first and then you will be able to do the schoolwork. No one can make you into a successful student unless you do it on your own.

Julio has shared his story. What will your story be? Will you recognize the behavioral or learning problems you currently have? Will you accept the responsibility for continuing to improve yourself? Getting into a regular education school does not mean that this work ends for you. In fact, the work of self-improvement and care can sometimes even be harder once you graduate into regular education classes. Owning your behavior, learning self-control, becoming a cooperator and gaining strong people skills are the tools you will need to make your dream happen. In the meantime, use your parents, school and friends to help you continue to make choices that help you and the other people around you feel safe and loved. Just because you have taken the time and learned to benefit from your special education program, you will not always be a passenger. Now you are ready to get in the driver's seat. Many special education students resist actively or passively the very programs that are supposed to help them. You have found a way to make the most of your school. We believe that any student who asks, "What will I learn today?" will be better off than the student who says, "You can't make me learn today." So go ahead and ride the big bus and wave goodbye to the cheese bus.

Appendix:

For a child's parent, guardian or advocate, understanding the technical and legal aspects of special education services can be time-consuming and confusing. This appendix is designed to give the reader a brief overview of reference-type information that will help in negotiating the "system" successfully. Hopefully the added information will also aid the individual in developing a more complete knowledge of the professional, educational and therapeutic terminology often used at various school meetings throughout the referral, placement and discharge/exit process in special education.

Frequently Asked Questions (FAQs):

1.) What is special education? Special education services are provided to students with disabilities through the development and implementation of individually specialized education programs. These individual education programs (IEPs) focus on giving the student with disabilities educational support services so that they have an equal chance to succeed in the classroom. The student's IEP is highly individualized and provided at no cost to the child and family by the local school system.

2.) Who qualifies for special education services? Students who qualify for special education services have disabilities that interfere with their educational performance (or academic success). The disabilities are defined by federal and state law and have specific criteria that must be met in order for a student to receive special education services.

3.) What testing criterion is used to determine whether a child is eligible for special education services? In order for a student to qualify for special education services, they must have a disability. Different assessment tests are used to determine if a student has a disability and, if so, focus on determining what type of disability is present (e.g., mental retardation, a learning disability or behavioral disorder, to name only a few).

4.) What does the term "educational impact" mean? Educational impact refers to the influence a student's disability has on the ability to perform and achieve in the classroom.

5.) What are some of the services offered to a child in need once they enter special education? Children with disabilities can be offered a variety of services including, but not limited to, modified instruction in the classroom, provision of related services such as speech, language, physical and occupational therapies and coordination and monitoring of the student's IEP, to name a few.

6.) If a child qualifies for special education services, is their participation voluntary or required by law? Children and their parents have a choice whether to take advantage of special education services. In this sense, participation is voluntary.

7.) How long do children typically remain in special education programs? Students who qualify for special education services may access them till age twenty-one. Each year there is an annual review of the student's IEP. Every three years the student's eligibility for special education services is reviewed by the IEP team.

8.) Will the "special ed" label follow the child forever? Special education records are kept on file but only authorized staff and parents have access to them. Remember, all services are provided with the continued approval of the parent or guardian of the child.

9.) Who pays for the child's special education program? An appropriate public education is the right of each student. Special education services are paid for by the local school board, the state and with federal funds that accompany the educational mandates.

10.) How are children transported to and from a special education program each school day? The local public school system must provide transportation to special education programs as they would for any student in a neighborhood public school.

11.) What are the advantages of a child being in a special education program outside their "home school"? Special education programs that require intensive professional staffing have more supports to offer students. Related services such as group and individual therapy, help for speech and language, and occupational therapy are available in house in special education schools. These services are integrated into student's school routine.

12.) Why can't my home school provide needed special education services to my child? Children require different levels of intervention to address learning and behavioral problems. Home schools provide lower intensity services for special education students within their programs. A small number of special education students need more intensive programs. It makes educational and fiscal sense to pool resources within a community where they are most needed, in order to provide quality programs for all students.

Glossary of Terms:

IEP (Individual Education Program): The official educational plan, including related services, that meets the least restrictive, minimum needs of a student with special needs. It is the guiding document for evaluating the educational program of a student annually. The program is developed through the collaboration of teachers, parents and students. Accepting or rejecting special education services via the IEP is a voluntary process.

ITP (Individualized Transition Plan): This plan describes the steps you will take as you leave a special education program and re-enter a community school or graduate from high school. This plan is usually finalized at your IEP annual review meeting. For students, 14 years and older, this plan is required as part of their IEP. A transition plan is aimed at helping you to live safely and productively in your community and to use your experience most effectively after you leave your special education placement. This plan will be practical helping you move from school to work to living independently in your community. The adults in your life will sit down with you and look ahead to see what your needs are and how to best meet them when developing your ITP.

Disability Codes: Different handicapping conditions are given different service codes. For example, in some state counties the code for a learning disability would be 09 while an emotional disturbance would be coded 06.

Inclusion/Mainstreaming: A process which by law requires special education students to be included in regular education classes whenever beneficial to the child.

FAPE: The legal provision that requires all children be entitled to a free, appropriate, public education. FAPE is the legal foundation of existing special education placements.

Cooperative Learning: A teaching technique grouping approximately 2-6 students together as a way to assist one another in accomplishing an instructional or educational goal in the classroom.

Group Therapy: The structured, supervised interaction of a small number of students under the leadership of a trained helping professional. Because in real life we all live and work in groups, this type of therapy is fundamental to a strong therapeutic program for school-age children.

Individual Therapy: The private relationship between a trained helping professional and the identified client; in this case, the student.

Therapy: In a school setting, therapy is provided as an intervention by a trained helping professional to facilitate the emotional health and social and academic skill development.

Alternative Therapy: Additional activities in a school's program that offer opportunities for interpersonal development. Examples include short-term music therapy, art therapy, dance therapy and field trips to cultural events.

Psychologist: A trained helping professional who assesses and gives direction for treatment and interventions in an educational setting. This individual may offer individual and group therapy in addition to testing students as needed.

Child and Adolescent Psychiatrist: A trained medical professional who also has an expertise in psychology. Additionally, this professional specifically diagnoses and treats the emotional and behavioral needs of children.

Social Worker: A trained helping professional with a variety of skills including, but not limited to, the ability to diagnose, provide individual, group and family counseling, case management, and conduct home visits for treatment purposes.

Printed in the United States
34627LVS00006B/439-573

9 781413 788433